Isle of Man TT
The Golden Years
1913-1939
VOLUME ONE

Isle of Man TT *The Golden Years* 1913-1939

Contents

Photographing the
TT's formative years..........................4

1913 – 1915 12

1920 – 1923 22

1924 – 1926 30

1931 – 1932 38

1933 48

1935 60

1936 69

1937 78

1938 82

1939 88

Left: Jimmy Simpson sweeps through Hilberry in 1934. It was his last TT meeting, in which he took a richly-deserved win.

Photographing the TT's formative years

Norton's victorious team in the 1932 Senior. Stanley Woods (27) won, from

PHOTOGRAPHY was in its infancy when in 1862 Thomas Keig (pronounced Keg) set up a studio in Douglas on his native Isle of Man. Its main business was portraiture, for which Mr Keig won gold medals in exhibitions on the English mainland and this continued when Thomas Stanley Keig took over on the death of his father. However, a tremendous upsurge of the Island's tourist trade combined with the development of relatively portable cameras at the turn of the century saw postcard and souvenir photography becoming Keig's mainstay.

A new business opportunity arose when the Tourist Trophy motorcycle races, first run in 1907, moved from a public roads circuit on the western side of the island to the much more demanding Mountain Course in 1911. Thomas Keig spent practice periods and race days photographing competitors with their machines. From 1920 his main hunting ground was the busy paddock and start/finish area at its new site beside Glencrutchery Road on the outskirts of the Island's main town Douglas. Sometimes riders were also photographed at their team headquarters elsewhere in Douglas. Glass negative plates from Mr Keig's cumbersome mahogany and brass bellows camera were printed up, often overnight, and sold in postcard format to race fans and tourists.

In the mid-1920s, Stanley R Keig took over running his father's business and greatly expanded its range of services. However, the TT photography continued and as equipment became more sophisticated during the 1930s there was more on-course shooting from vantage points near Douglas such as Governor's Bridge or Quarterbridge and sometimes further afield.

Photographing the TT's formative years

Jimmy Guthrie (22) and Jimmy Simpson.

The photos in this book, spanning the years from 1913 to 1939 with a gap from 1928 to 1931, present a superb record of greater and lesser TT aces with machines that developed hugely over the years. Perhaps inevitably, the Tourist concept of competing with standard production motorcycles was soon left behind as manufacturers vied for the prestige of TT success.

The spindly bicycle-like machines of early years can be seen to develop into specialised road racers with large fuel tanks, a liberal use of light alloys and hydraulic suspension. Riding kit evolves from a miscellany of protective clothing to purpose-made suits of strong hide, while the photos also offer insight into social history. Bystanders, in the quaint-looking clothing of the day, add charm to many of the images and schoolboys packing the paddock looking for autographs loved to get in the picture with their TT heroes. Long before television and computer games the noisy, smelly excitement provided by the Glencrutchery Road paddock must have been irresistible to many boys and some girls. In some early photos, blurred faces are evidence of long exposure times: the main subjects were probably asked to hold very still.

Atmosphere is also conveyed by the group shots taken of riders with their jubilant supporters after a win or high placing, as well as by on-course views showing crowds of spectators.

A lack of brilliant sunshine in many of the paddock shots doesn't necessarily reflect of the Isle of Man's climate. Before World War Two almost all practice sessions took place in the early morning, the first evening session being introduced in 1937.

Isle of Man TT *The Golden Years*

Photographing the TT's formative years

Start of the 1921 350cc Junior race on Glencrutchery Road before the gigantic scoreboard was built five years later.

Not surprisingly, given the great age of the original negatives, some photos show evidence of damage. For speed and ease of cataloguing in Keig's commercial operation, caption information was inscribed directly on plates and sometimes overlaps the subject. It is noticeable that the photographer often focused on the rider, rather than his motorcycle, in many of the paddocks shots. Photo editing software has made it possible for painstaking re-touchers to make good the worst of the damage and in most cases remove inscriptions made by Keig staff, now made redundant by the captions.

The format of the TT races changed considerably during the years covered here. However, the Junior and Senior events, for machines of up to 350cc and 500cc respectively, were staged throughout the period and remained in the programme in that form until the 1980s. The premier Senior race, run over seven laps in 1913, was reduced to six laps until a seventh lap was re-introduced in 1926. The Junior was a five-lapper until it gained another lap in 1923 then joined the Senior in having seven laps from 1926.

Freddie Frith on his 350cc Norton in 1937. It has a detachable silencer fitted in the exhaust megaphone for legal riding on open roads.

Photographing the TT's formative years

An award for the best 250cc rider in the Junior was instigated for 1920 and two years later quarter-litre machines, which were enjoying a sales boom, got their own five-lap Lightweight race, lengthened to six laps in 1923 and seven in the 1926 shake-up. A 250cc Lightweight race would be retained until 1977, when it was renamed the Junior 250cc.

Races for motorcycles with sidecars were run from 1923 to 1925. While spectators loved seeing the unstable outfits at speed, the retail trade feared that a daredevil image would affect the sales of sidecars as economy family transport.

An Ultra-Lightweight race for machines up to 175cc was introduced as a three-lapper in 1924 and extended to four laps in the following year before being dropped. The class would be revived in 1951 with a 125cc upper limit.

In the early years of the Mountain, not all of Britain's then-numerous manufacturers were enthusiastic about the arduous and dangerous TT, but by the mid-1920s many were involved and a few emerged as prominent contenders, like AJS, Douglas, Excelsior, New Imperial, Norton, Rudge and Velocette. The original concept of an endurance race for standard showroom machines had been long forgotten and an elite class of riders was supplied with factory bikes having much higher performance than was available to privateers. The TT

Right top: Ted Mellors with the 350cc factory Velocette he rode to fourth in the 1939 Junior TT.

Right: A crowd gathers round Douggie Alexander's Royal Enfield. He had finished the 1914 Junior TT despite losing his saddle on the second lap of five.

Isle of Man TT *The Golden Years*

First rider away in the 1933 Junior, Alec Mitchell pushes off his Velocette.

Photographing the TT's formative years

became more truly international, being joined in the calendar by Continental Grand Prix events and British firms, once supreme, faced increasing pressure from foreign makes. During the run-up to World War Two TT races were won by BMW and DKW of Germany as well as Moto Guzzi of Italy.

The most successful TT riders (two or more wins) 1911-1939

Ten wins: Stanley Woods
Six: Jimmy Guthrie
Four: Freddie Frith
Two: Charlie Dodson, Eddie Twemlow, Eric Williams, Freddie Dixon, Howard Davies, Jock Porter, Tim Hunt, Tom Sheard

Wins by manufacturer 1911-1939

Norton 18, AJS 6, New Imperial, Rudge and Velocette 5, Douglas and Sunbeam 4, Moto Guzzi and Rex Acme 3, Cotton, Excelsior, HRD, New Gerrard, Scott 2, Benelli, BMW, DKW, Indian, Levis, OK Supreme 1
Prior to 1939 the most outright lap records were broken by Jimmy Simpson, first rider to lap at over 60mph, 70mph and 80mph. They were as follows:
1924 Junior 64.54mph
1925 Senior 68.97mph
1926 Senior 70.43mph
1931 Senior 80.82mph
1932 Senior 81.50mph

The outright lap record standing when World War Two broke out was 91.00mph, set by Harold Daniell on a Norton in winning the 1938 Senior TT.

Isle of Man TT *The Golden Years*

1913–1915

Local rider Douggie Brown (left) A Lindsay and C Newsome pose for the camera on the TT Course just beyond the Quarterbridge Hotel. They comprise the Rover factory team, winners of a Manufacturers' Team Award introduced in 1913. Rover made motorcycles until 1925, then concentrated on four-wheelers. In 1913 only, the Junior and Senior races were in two legs, run on separate days.

1913–1915

Above: In 1914, the start/finish area was moved from Quarterbridge Road to the top of Bray Hill, with a temporary row of pits, literally dug in the ground, alongside the road and a grandstand behind. Riders arrived along Ballanard Road to make a sharp right turn at St Ninian's church. Here Oliver Godfrey starts the Senior race in which he took second place on an Indian. Less than half of the 111 starters finished.

Left: Dead heats are rare in TT history but in the 1914 Senior Oliver Godfrey, seen here with his Indian, tied for second place with Sunbeam rider Howard Davies. Godfrey had won the 1911 Senior, leading the sensational 1-2-3 victory for the red American V-twins with two-speed countershaft gearboxes and all-chain drive. This would be Godfrey's last TT: during World War One he was killed serving in the Royal Flying Corps.

Bert Colver at the Matchless pit during the 1914 Senior race. Gear selection problems dropped him from second place to fourth. Fellow Matchless riders Charlie and Harry Collier, both seen as likely winners, both retired. The Chase pit next to Colliers is empty: the London manufacturer's rider Vaughan Knight fell off at Bray Hill on the first lap, causing a four-minute delay for following riders.

1913 – 1915

Left: Employed at the Sunbeam factory in Wolverhampton, Tommy de la Hay rode this side-valve 499cc three-speed single to 13th place in the windswept 1914 Senior. A reserve, he took over the ride after regular factory teamster Charlie Nokes had a minor heart attack and was not fit to race. In 1920 De la Hay won the Senior and, jointly with Norton rider Douggie Brown would set the first 50mph race average. .

Right: Bill Sheard aboard one of nine Royal Enfields with Swiss-made V-twin engines entered in the 1914 Junior. Frank Walker finished third on one, but apparently concussed after a spill, he rode into a barrier at St Ninian's and died from his injuries. Sheard, wearing a helmet, as made mandatory in 1914, finished 26th. Bill should not be confused with two-times TT winner Tom Sheard.

The progressive AJS factory of Wolverhampton dominated the 1914 Junior with side-valve singles equipped with two-speed gearboxes and twin primary chains to provide four ratios. Here winner Eric Williams completes the five laps, over which he averaged 45.58mph and raised the lap record to 47.57mph despite rain and Mountain mist. His AJS team namesake Cyril Williams was second.

1913 – 1915

Dapper Howard R Davies on his Junior AJS, a factory entry with an advanced overhead valve engine. A puncture robbed him of victory, which went to team-mate Eric Williams, but Davies made history by winning the Senior race with a Junior-size 350cc engine. Trained in engineering at AJS, he tied for second in the 1914 Senior on a Sunbeam and served as a World War One despatch rider before returning to AJS.

Bert Le Vack was a member of the Indian equipe that won the Senior Team Prize in the 1921 Senior, finishing third behind team-mate Freddie Dixon. Both were 10 minutes faster than the previous year's winner. Le Vack, who had recorded 107.5mph on one of Indian's 'half twin' side-valve singles at Brooklands prior to the TT, was a great speed rider who rarely enjoyed good luck on the Island.

Despite only racing twice, Walter Brandish is immortalised in TT history by Brandish Corner between Creg-ny-Baa and Hilberry, so named because the Coventry rider fell off there while practising in 1923, breaking a leg. This shot is of him on the Rover he rode to 13th place in the 1921 Senior. In the following year he was second on a four-valve Ricardo Triumph.

1913 – 1915

Right: TT debutant Londoner Frank Longman finished 34th in the 1921 Junior on this Wooler ohv flat-twin with belt drive, averaging 34.4mph. Brainchild of London-based John Wooler, the machine had an unusually long cream-yellow and black fuel tank, that led to it being nick-named The Flying Banana. Longman, who won two European championships, the 350cc in 1926 and 250cc in 1929, died after crashing in the 1933 Lightweight TT.

Left: In 1920 and 1921, The Motor Cycle Cup was awarded for the highest finisher in a 250cc Lightweight class run within the 350cc Junior. Won by Ronald Clark on a two-stroke Levis in the first year, the 1921 victor was Doug Prentice, seen here on his four-stroke New Imperial. He finished 10th overall at an average of 44.80mph. Birmingham's progressive New Imperial factory won a total of five Lightweight TTs and one Junior.

Isle of Man TT *The Golden Years*

Looking along Glencrutchery road during the start of the 1921 Junior. Number 24 is eventual 250cc class winner Prentice and Number 28 is the veteran rider 59 year old Frank 'Pa' Applebee on a Levis. A Londoner, he had competed in the first Tourist Trophy race of 1907, as had his son Frank Jnr, winner of the 1912 Senior on a Scott.

1913 – 1915

1920-1923

Bert Le Vack was a member of the Indian equipe that won the Senior Team Prize in the 1921 Senior, finishing third behind team-mate Freddie Dixon. Both were 10 minutes faster than the previous year's winner. Le Vack, who had recorded 107.5mph on one of Indian's 'half twin' side-valve singles at Brooklands prior to the TT, was a great speed rider who rarely enjoyed good luck on the Island.

Bert Le Vack ready to start in the 1922 Junior, which he led by two minutes at a record speed of 56.46mph on lap three, before retiring with gearbox trouble. His New Imperial has a 344cc double overhead camshaft engine, the first in the TT, which he developed in eight weeks for his new employer, engine-maker JAP (JA Prestwich). With him is ACU steward Archibald Low, a visionary inventor who pioneered rocketry and a form of television.

After finishing second in the 1921 Senior on an Indian, Freddie Dixon failed to finish on this machine in 1922. Dixon is pictured in a quarry near Douglas harbour where his team was based.

1920-1923

Tynesider J Joynson's 250cc Invicta only survived four laps of the five-lap 1922 Lightweight race. The machine was made by Arthur Barnett and Gordon Francis, who went on to found the Coventry-based Francis-Barnett marque, which survived until the 1960s, by which time it specialised in sporting and commuter lightweight two-strokes.

Isle of Man TT *The Golden Years*

A race for sidecar outfits introduced in 1923 proved popular with spectators. You can see why from this shot of Graham Walker rounding a crowded Ramsey Hairpin on his 600cc Norton with his intrepid passenger hanging out to keep the Hughes sidecar's wheel down. Norton's team manager Walker finished second behind Freddie Dixon's Douglas, after early leader Harry Langman's lurid driving ended in a crash.

1920-1923

The distinctive profile of the low-slung water-cooled two-stroke Scott twin is obvious in this shot of Howard Riddell. This is the 486cc Squirrel production model on which he took 18th place in the 1923 Senior. By the mid-Twenties Scott's best racing days were over: the inventive marque founder AA Scott had left the company in 1915 and died from pneumonia in July 1923.

1920-1923

After persuading Cotton to give him a ride in 1922, precocious teenager Stanley Woods finished fifth in the Junior, despite various mishaps including having his riding kit catch fire during a pit stop. In 1923 he won the Junior on this 350cc Blackburne-engined machine from the Gloucester factory, which built frames with triangulated straight tubes. A Dubliner, Woods was classed as a British rider, since the Irish Republic was not founded until 1949.

Isle of Man TT *The Golden Years*

Start of the 1922 Senior race, by the elevated timekeepers' office. Number 45 is Jock Porter, proprietor of Porter's Motor Mart in Edinburgh who built his own New Gerrard motorcycles with various engines. His 500cc Senior mount with a 482cc side-valve JAP V-twin engine was not as competitive as smaller bikes he rode to victory in the 1923 250cc Lightweight and the 1924 175cc Ultra Lightweight.

1920-1923

Left: By 1923, Indian's TT swansong contender was a 497cc side-valve single with an upright cylinder and side valves operated by twin camshafts. This is Freddie Dixon who finished third in the rain-lashed Senior, after the other Indian riders Frank Longman and RD Gelling retired. Ernest Bridgeman, head of Indian's UK operation, is standing by Dixon in trilby and bow tie.

Below: Cheshire's Syd Crabtree on the 500cc overhead valve AJS he rode into 13th place in the Senior of 1923, his second year at the TT. His helmet rests on a leather tool box mounted on top of the fuel tank, which is box-shaped as was typical at the time. Syd, who won several Continental Grands Prix as well as the 1929 Lightweight TT (on an Excelsior), was killed when he crashed in Mountain mist during the 1934 Lightweight.

One of 15 Nortons entered for the 1920 Senior was this 16H ridden by Vincent 'Vic' Horsman from Liverpool, who failed to finish. Contesting four TTs between 1913 and 1921, his best result was 13th on a Singer in his debut year. Horsman excelled at Brooklands where he took numerous speed records. In 1920 he averaged 72.48mph on a Norton for one hour and later helped Triumph develop racing engines.

1924–1926

Congratulations for 20 year old Kenneth Twemlow after his 1924 Junior victory on a standard JAP-engined New Imperial sports model. His brother Edwin won the Lightweight, also on a New Imperial and it was both riders' first attempt at the TT. Their father, boss of the Foden truck company, marked the family double by having his sons' race numbers set in mortar on a garage building being renovated on Douglas Promenade.

Above: Harry Langman's second place behind Alec Bennett's factory Norton in the 1924 Senior showed that the Yorkshire marque's unique twin was still competitive in the hands of an exceptional TT rider. Number 14 on the left is the New Imperial of Cheshire amateur George Tottey, a non-finisher in the Junior

Left: Alec Bennett gave the Sunbeam factory its first TT victory in the 1922 Senior, the last TT win by a side-valve engine. This is his long-serving team-mate Tommy De La Hay, who apparently resented demotion to Number Two factory rider behind freelancer Bennett. He finished sixth. TT rules revisions for 1926 made the use of petrol, rather than high-octane alcohol fuels, mandatory.

1924-1928

Sixty-one year old George 'Pa' Cowley was the oldest driver in the 1925 Sidecar TT. Passengered on a 350cc Sunbeam outfit by D Cowley (no relation), he failed to finish, as he had in 1924. Cowley Senior, who entered the 1914 TT but failed to qualify and was a non-starter due to a practice crash in 1920, was 19th in the 1922 Senior and 12th in the 1924 Junior.

Isle of Man TT *The Golden Years*

Winner of the 1908 Twin Cylinder TT on a Dot, Harry Reed stuck with the Mancunian brand throughout a long TT career lasting until 1925. Here Reed and his passenger J Hooson are on the 344cc JAP-engined Dot they took to second place in the 1924 Sidecar race, despite racing against 500cc and 600cc engines. The sidecar is by Swallow of Blackpool, co-founded by William Lyons, the man behind Jaguar cars.

South African CH Young finished fourth in the 1924 Senior on a Triumph single. Its four-valve engine, used in road and racing machines, was developed for Triumph by research engineers Harry Ricardo and Frank Halford who both achieved fame in the world of aviation. In Motor Cycling speed traps, Young was the fastest 500 on the Mountain climb (50.5mph) and descent (72mph). On Sulby Straight, he was 7th fastest at 75mph, Scott rider CH Wood being quickest at 80.35mph.

When Howard Raymond Davies took his second Senior win, it was on a machine of his own HRD brand. After involvement with AJS and Sunbeam, Davies set up his own factory in Wolverhampton to build machines, initially with JAP engines. The 1925 Senior victory came after Jimmy Simpson raised the record to 69mph on his AJS before retiring. In 1928 Philip Vincent bought out HRD to found Vincent-HRD in Stevenage.

1924-1928

Jock Porter won the 1923 Lightweight and the 1924 175cc Ultra Lightweight, but was less successful in the 1925 Senior on this bigger version of his self-built New Gerrard with a 482cc JAP side-valve V-twin engine. Seen here rounding a sunny, tree-less Governor's Dip, Porter retired on the third lap. New Gerrard production continued until World War Two.

Before he became a car racing legend, Achille Varzi raced motorcycles and was a TT competitor from 1924 to 1927, returning for a final ride in 1930 by which time he was one of Italy's top drivers on four wheels. Here he sits on the 350cc Dot with an oil-cooled Bradshaw engine on which he failed to finish on his debut in the 1924 Junior His best result was fifth in the 1927 Lightweight on a Moto Guzzi.

Twenty year old Len Parker, who rode for the Douglas factory in his home city of Bristol, crosses the line with passenger Ken Horstman to win the four-lap 1925 Sidecar race ahead of the Norton pairings of Bert Taylor/Charlie Hirst and George Grinton/Arthur Kinrade.

Left: Freddie Dixon and passenger Tom Denny emerge from Governor's Dip on their 596cc Douglas outfit with an ingeniously hinged sidecar body banked over by a lever to enable faster cornering. Sidecar winner in 1923, Dixon set the fastest lap in the next two years but didn't finish. His 1925 record of 57.18mph would stand until the next Mountain Course Sidecar race was run in 1960, when Helmut Fath's 500cc BMW lapped at 85.79mph.

1924-1928

Third in the first Sidecar TT in 1923 and winner in 1924, George Tucker failed to finish on this 588cc Norton/Hughes outfit in 1925. Here he poses with passenger G Hammond, who replaced Norton employee Walter Moore for Tucker's third TT. (Moore designed Norton's first overhead camshaft engine, winner of the 1927 Senior). Disliked by the motorcycle trade, the sidecar TT was abandoned after 1925, but revived on the Clypse circuit in 1953.

Isle of Man TT *The Golden Years*

The New Hudson team show off overhead valve 500cc machines designed by Bert Le Vack (third from left), who had recently joined the Birmingham factory. In the Senior Austin Harris rode Number 50 and Oliver Langton rode 45, but neither finished, reflecting a lack of preparation time. In the 1927 Senior, however, rising star Jimmy Guthrie would ride a New Hudson to second place.

1924-1928

Arriving from Italy, Luigi Arcangeli expressed at amazement at the difficulty of TT Course. In his first year he rode this blue 348cc Bianchi Freccia Celeste (Sky Arrow) with an advanced double overhead camshaft engine to a creditable 14th place in the Junior. In 1927 he took second place in the Lightweight on a 250cc Motor Guzzi and in 1928 he rode a British Sunbeam to 15th in the Senior.

1931-1932

Riding from 1924, former marine engineer Harold Willis joined Velocette in 1927 a year after the factory's first TT win. He introduced many improvements including revolutionary foot-operated gearchange for 1928, the year of Velo's second TT win and later swinging arm rear suspension. A humorist who coined his own vocabulary of motorcycling words, Willis sits on his 11th-placed 1931 Junior machine and talks to TT medical officer Dr Letchworth.

The first Senior-Junior double winner Percy 'Tim' Hunt. In winning the 1928 Amateur TT, he sensationally beat the absolute TT lap record lap by two seconds, at 67.94mph. With Norton from 1930 to 1933, Hunt was the first team rider to use a twistgrip throttle instead of a lever. He is seen here with his Senior bike on which he raised the lap record to 75.27mph. This was the first TT success for Norton's latest ohc engine, designed by Arthur Carroll and Joe Craig.

Raleigh of Nottingham entered three machines in the 1931 Senior. Their 495cc engines had crankcases of magnesium alloy, also used to house the Raleigh-made Sturmey Archer four-speed gearboxes. A 'saddle' style of fuel tank, as adopted by most makers from around 1930, was fitted. The rider is Loughborough's Arthur Tyler, only finisher of the three in seventh place. He also raced at the Donington Park circuit, opened in 1931.

Isle of Man TT *The Golden Years*

1931-1932

Special guest Prince George (later Duke of Kent) meets Walter Handley, one of the favourites, on the start line before the 1932 Senior TT. The Prince, uncle to the current Queen, enjoyed a scandalous sex-and-drugs lifestyle and died in an air crash in 1942. What the man on the right is doing is anyone's guess.

41

Isle of Man TT *The Golden Years*

Jimmy Simpson at Governor's Bridge in the 1932 Senior. He and Norton team-mates Stanley Woods and Jimmy Guthrie had orders to race for three laps, then hold positions. Believing Simpson was expected to win, Woods chased him down, got ahead on lap three and won. Guthrie took

1931-1932

second place after Simpson's clutch began to slip. Woods had won the Junior and Norton became the first factory to take a 1-2-3 double in both the Senior and Junior TT's.

Isle of Man TT *The Golden Years*

Jimmy Simpson was Mr Lap Record: the first TT rider to hoist the outright lap record above 60mph (1924 Junior), 70mph (1926 Senior) and 80mph (1931 Senior). He broke lap records in eight TT races but won only one, the 1934 250cc Lightweight. Here he sits on his 1932 Junior overhead camshaft factory Norton, which like many of hard-riding Simpson's machines, did not last the race.

1931-1932

Left: Vic Brittain, father of postwar trials ace John Brittain, was 13th in the 1932 Senior on this Sunbeam.

Below: Two Junior Velocette entrants in 1932: Coventry-born Ernie Thomas (left) and Alec Mitchell from Huddersfield. Thomas rode in 18 international TTs after a non-finish in the 1927 Amateur TT, his best result being third in the 1937 lightweight on a German DKW. Mitchell's brother Hirst had given up racing after his third TT in the previous year. Schoolboys loved to pose in Keig's paddock photos when not collecting autographs.

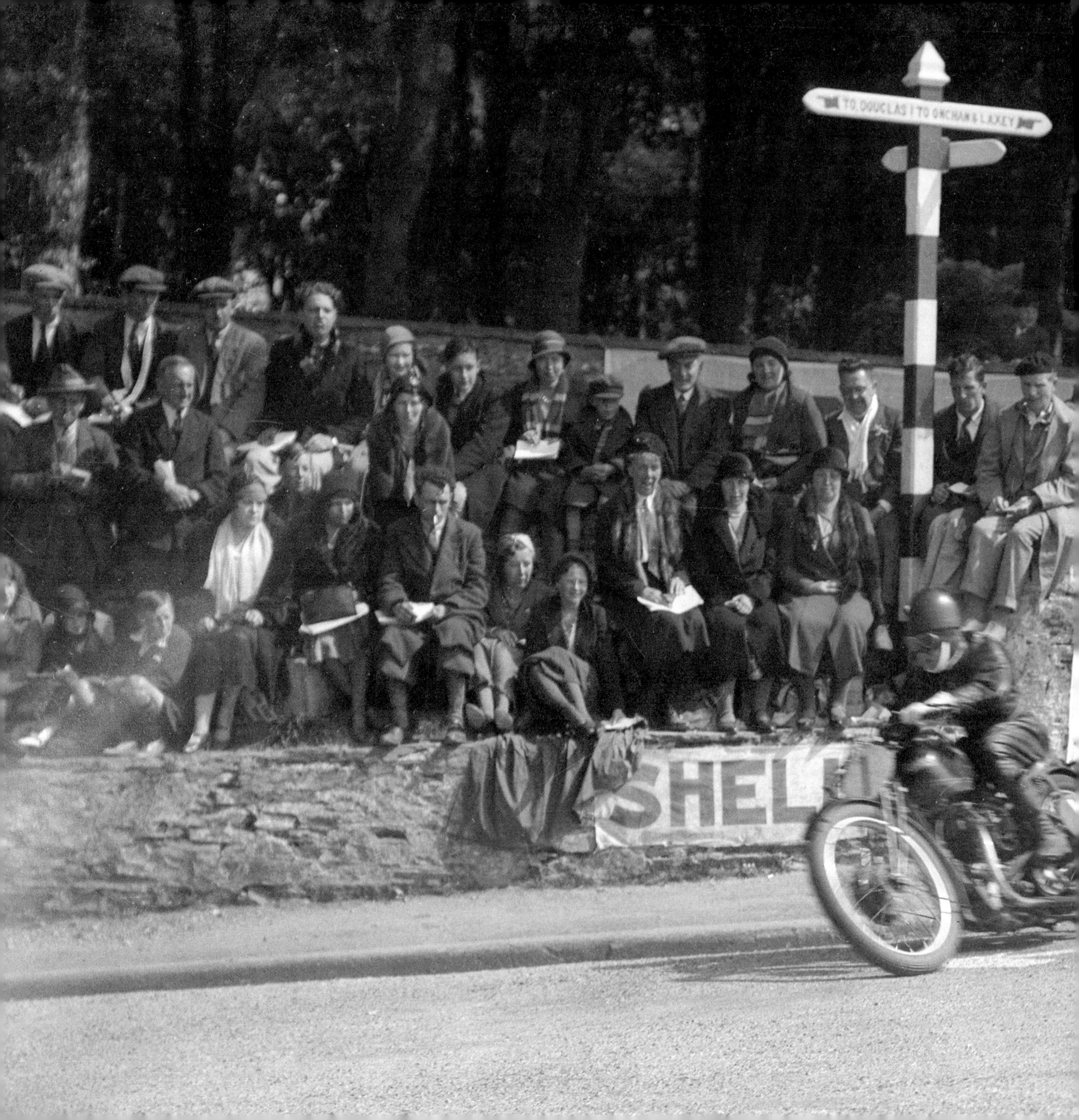
SHEL

1931-1932

Fearless Wal Handley was one of the first TT heroes to attract a large fan base. He won four races, including a Lightweight-Junior double in 1925, but had his share of disappointments. Here he rounds Governor's Bridge in the 1932 Senior: he was holding third place on his Rudge behind Nortons when he crashed on the Z-bend just after the 11th Milestone, later permanently named Handley's Corner.

47

1933

Above left: Sunbeam made its first foray into the Lightweight class with its 250cc 'Little 90' (the Model 90 was the company's super-sporting 500cc flagship). This one is ridden by long-time Sunbeam campaigner Gilbert Emery who retired on the third of seven laps. Two other Little 90 riders, Eddie Hughes and Ted Merrill, both crashed.

Above right: Wal Handley, here with the Velocette KTT on which he finished seventh in the 1933 Junior, had a difficult TT that year. Torn between Moto Guzzi and the latest Excelsior for the Lightweight he chose the latter, but suffered a mysterious lack of power. He didn't start in the Senior, deeming his OK-Supreme JAP too slow. Velocette won the Junior team prize, with six KTTs in the top ten finishers.

Left: Irish rider CW 'Paddy' Johnston was a friend of Stanley Woods and had an even longer TT career. First racing in 1922, Johnston won the 1926 Lightweight on a Cotton, the make he is seen with here in 1933, when he was a Lightweight non-finisher. Second in the 1930 Lightweight on an OK Supreme, he raced on in postwar TTs, finishing in the Lightweight and Junior of 1947 and the first 125cc TT of 1951.

1933

Easily identified by yellow and black striped riding gear, Tommy Spann rode for the Czechoslovakian Jawa factory in the 1933 Senior. His machine, with an ohv single engine, weighed only 120kg (265lb) and was designed by English engineer and TT rider George Patchett who joined Jawa in 1930. Spann finished 12th, four places behind team-mate Stanley 'Ginger' Wood. A third Jawa rider, F Brand, retired on lap four.

Mario Ghersi, younger brother of 1926 Lightweight hero Pietro, was a fancied runner in the 1933 Lightweight on the latest ohc Moto Guzzi. But in the seven-lap race for 250cc machines, the Italian had to settle for sixth behind British machines, more than 3mph down on winner Syd Gleave's Excelsior. Standing behind the bike is the other Guzzi rider, three-times Italian champion Terzo Bandini, who did not finish the race. .

1933

Italian enthusiast Eduardo Self on the 500cc Ganna made in his home town of Varese that he rode in the 1933 Senior. He also rode a 350cc machine of the same make in the Junior but failed to finish in either race. Self had made his TT debut the previous year, when he finished 11th in the Junior on a Velocette.

Three of the dominant Norton team's stars: Jimmy Simpson (15), Percy 'Tim' Hunt (25) and double winner Stanley Woods on 500cc Senior machines. Simpson was second in the race, followed in by Hunt and fourth team member Jimmy Guthrie, while Woods' pushed the lap record to 82.74mph. Dowty's photo business in the background was bought out by Keig.

1933

Irish rider CW 'Paddy' Johnston was a friend of Stanley Woods and had an even longer TT career. First racing in 1922, Johnston won the 1926 Lightweight on a Cotton, the make he is seen with here in 1933, when he was a Lightweight non-finisher. Second in the 1930 Lightweight on an OK Supreme, he raced on in postwar TTs, finishing in the Lightweight and Junior of 1947 and the first 125cc TT of 1951.

Lightweight winner Syd Gleave with the Excelsior nicknamed the Mechanical Marvel. Its HJ Hatch-designed single-cylinder Blackburne engine had twin overhead camshafts with four radial valves, twin carburettors and twin exhausts. Gleave fought strong winds to take victory in the seven-lap race at a record average of 71.59mph. Sid Crabtree was fifth on another Marvel, but Wal Handley failed to finish on his. Despite its advanced features, the design was not developed further.

From Hawick in the Scottish borders, Jimmy Guthrie served at Gallipoli and on the Western Front in World War One. First with Norton for 1928, he rode AJS in 1930, winning in the Lightweight TT. Here poses near the team's Castle Mona Hotel base on his Senior machine. The Motor Cycle said of the stoical Guthrie: 'as soon as he gets astride a motorcycle he goes all crackers'.

1934

An early example of an iconic Mountain Course photo location: at the sharp Creg-ny-Baa right-hander looking back at the descent from Keppel Gate. This shows Jimmy Simpson (Norton), just ahead of another rider, on his way to second place behind Guthrie in the Junior. He went on to take his first TT win in the lightweight and collect another second place in the Senior.

Velocette's team for the Junior, out of their leathers. Left: Harold Lamacraft, right: Gilbert Emery and middle: Les Archer a prominent Brooklands rider whose son Les Junior was Britain's top motocross star in the 1950s. Velocette's overhead camshaft KTT engine filled seven of the top ten places.

1933

A lovely action shot of Wal Handley on his 350cc Norton in Monday's sun-drenched Junior, watched at Hilberry by a lone spectator. When lying third behind team-mates Guthrie and Simpson, he fell at Governor's Bridge on lap five, depriving Norton of a 1-2-3 with its new all-alloy engine. Facial injuries prevented Walter from riding in Friday's Senior in which his team mates to a second 1-2.

Triumph returned with a 500cc single, the Valentine Page-designed 5/10 with a large plum-coloured fuel tank. This is team reserve Allan Jefferies, father of 1971 F750 TT winner Tony Jefferies and 1993 Formula 1 winner Nick Jefferies. Tony's son David was the legendary winner of nine TTs from 1999 to 2002. Allan did not race and none of the three Triumph starters finished.

Cheerful despite grim weather, Jimmy Simpson prepares to start his Rudge in Wednesday's Lightweight. 'Unlucky Jim' achieved his sole TT win in this race at his last TT. Out of 24 starters in this race only eight finished. Several riders fell off in Mountain fog, including 1929 Lightweight winner Syd Crabtree, who died from his injuries.

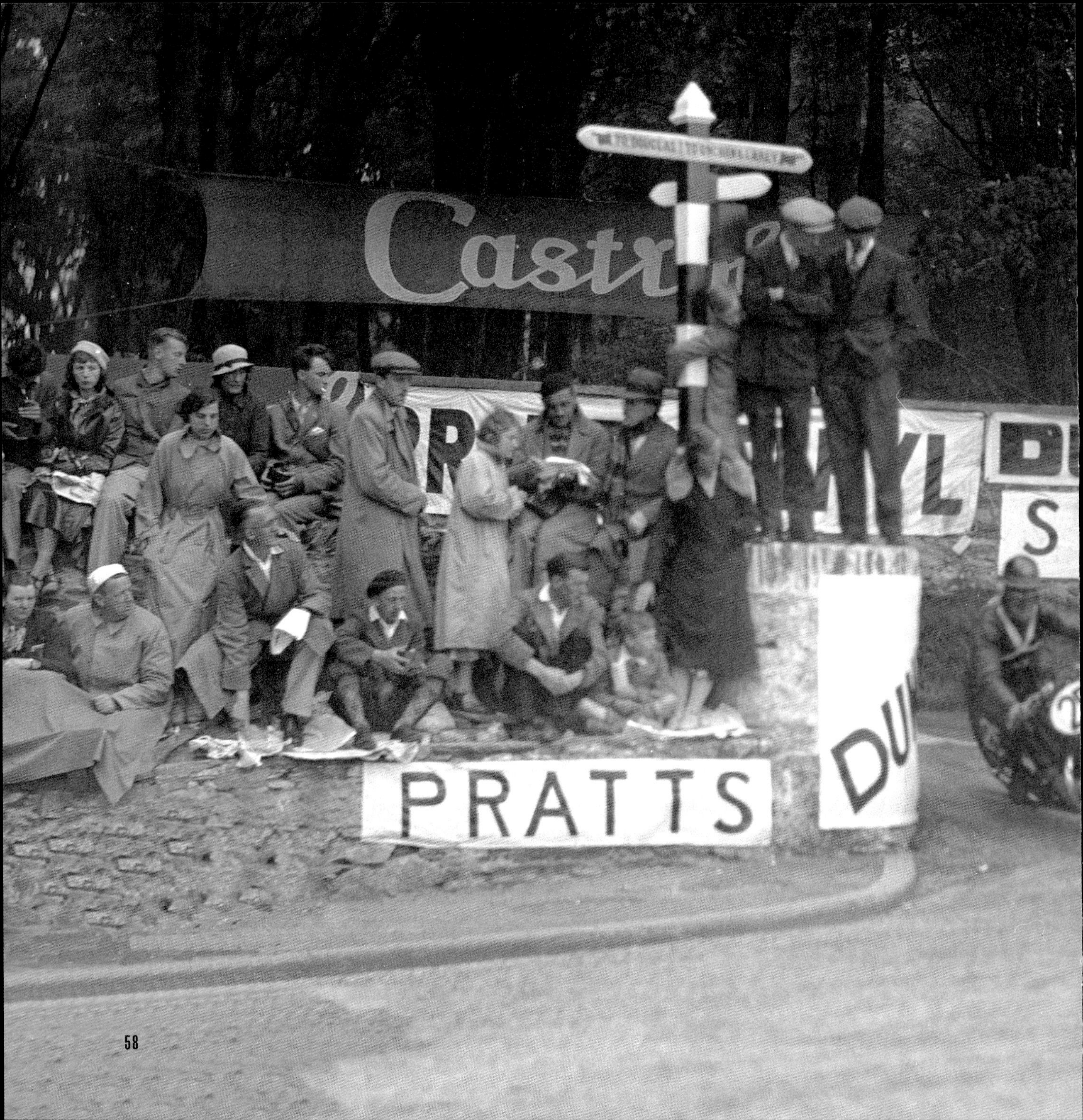
PRATTS

1933

Second rider home in the Lightweight, Ernie Nott cranks round the dead-slow Governor's Bridge Hairpin on his four-valve Rudge. He was followed in by fellow Rudge rider Graham Walker, who fended off Stanley Woods' Moto Guzzi by less than 30 seconds. Nott would finish third in the Junior on a Husqvarna, the Swedish marque's best result in eight TTs contested from 1931 to 1975.

1935

Right: After only one year with Norton in 1934, Wal Handley was back with Velocette in 1935. He practiced on this Junior machine until injuring a hand when reaching down to adjust the rear brake on Sulby Straight and was unable to race. His Velocette ride was offered to Stanley Woods, who criticised the machine after one practice lap but joined the team for 1936.

Jimmy Guthrie shakes hands with one of Norton's directors Bill Mansell and team chief Joe Craig (wearing armband) after winning the 1935 Junior. At that time Number 1 plates were given to the previous year's previous winners: Guthrie had won a Junior-Senior double in 1934.

1935

For the first time since 1911, the Senior was won by a foreign machine. Always seeking the best machines, Stanley Woods rode Moto Guzzi's advanced 120-degree ohc V-twin with rear springing to snatch victory from Norton star Jimmy Guthrie on the last lap. His pit attendant, in white overalls and getting a jubilant squeeze, was Manx resident Eric Brown, nephew of early TT racer Douggie Brown.

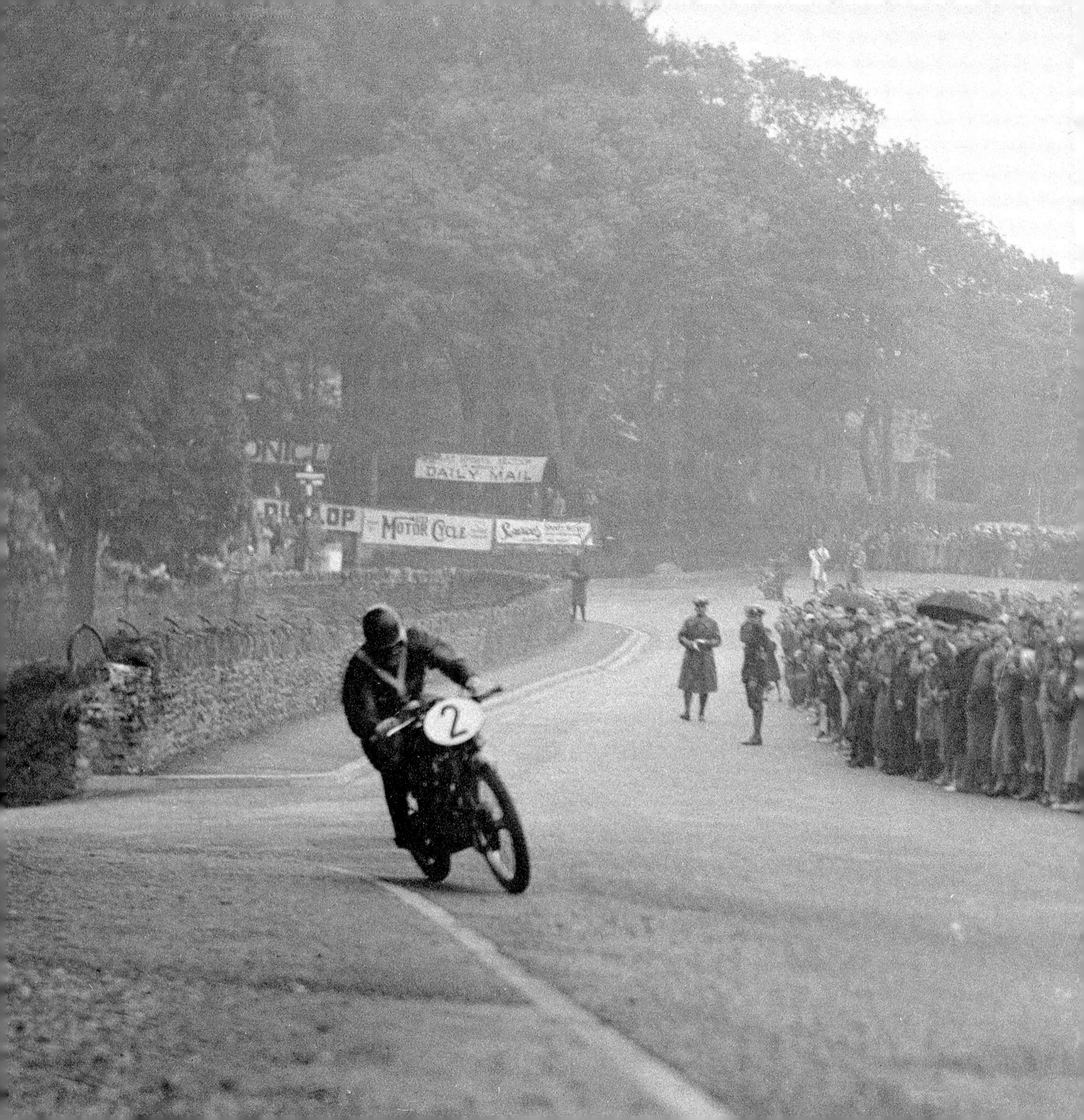
DAILY MAIL
MOTOR CYCLE

1935

Woods' first win of the week was in the Lightweight, on a Moto Guzzi that broke a valve rocker as he crossed the line. As seen in this shot of him exiting Governor's Dip, the weather was poor but even so, Stanley hoisted the lap record to 74.19mph. His main challengers were team-mate Omobono Tenni and New Imperial's Doug Pirie. The Italian fell at Creg-ny-Baa and 1934 Senior Manx GP winner Pirie crashed on the Mountain with fatal consequences.

Isle of Man TT *The Golden Years*

Ulsterman Walter Rusk, nicknamed the Blond Bombshell, took to the Mountain Course quickly, finishing third in the Senior on a Velocette in 1934, his second year. On factory Nortons in 1935, he was second in the Junior and third in the Senior, postponed from Friday to Saturday, but still held in poor weather. This is Rusk at Governor's Dip in the Senior.

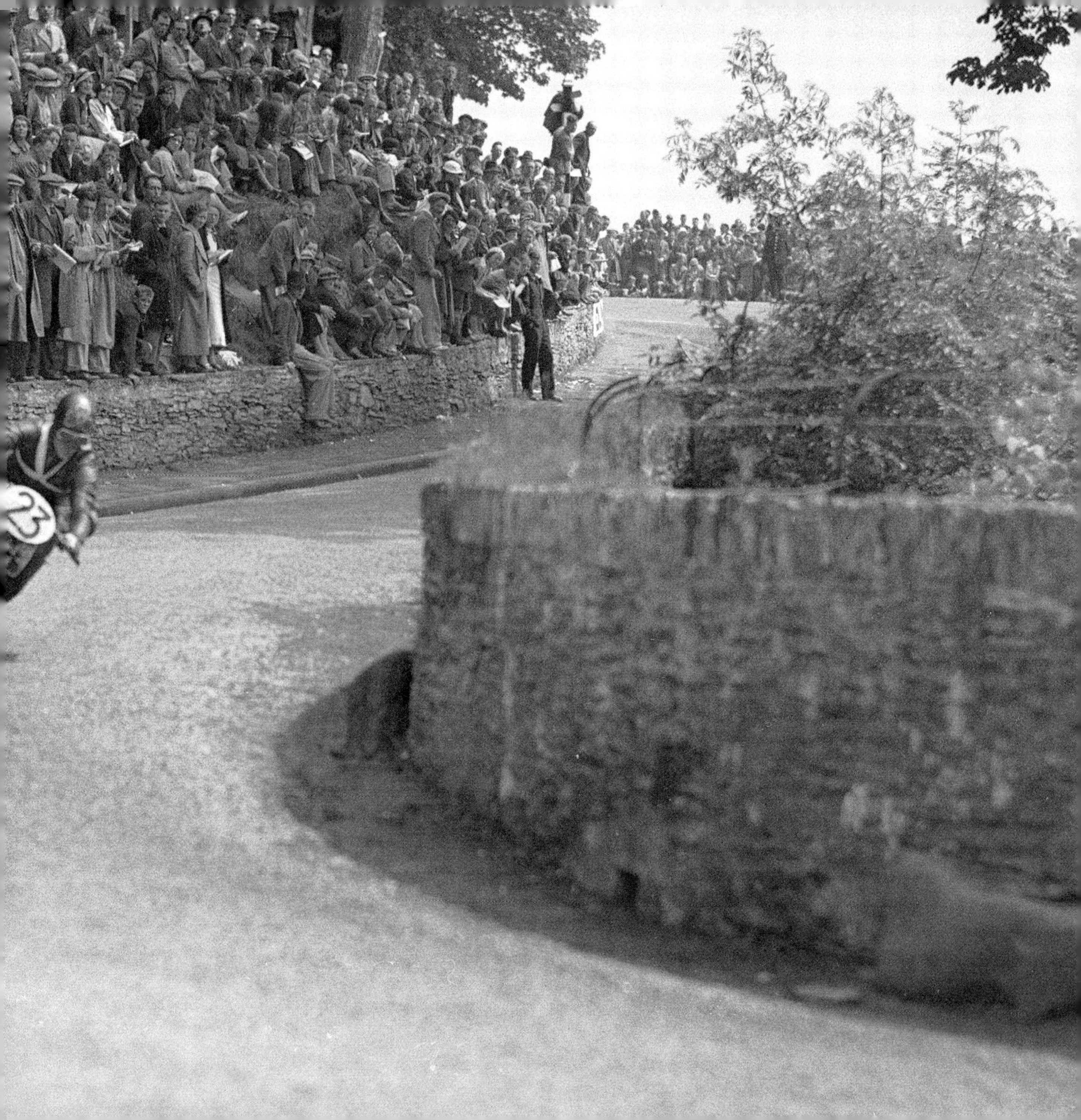
23

A shot taken looking down from the grandstand as 1935 Junior race competitors prepare for the start. The roadside refuelling pits can be seen in the foreground.

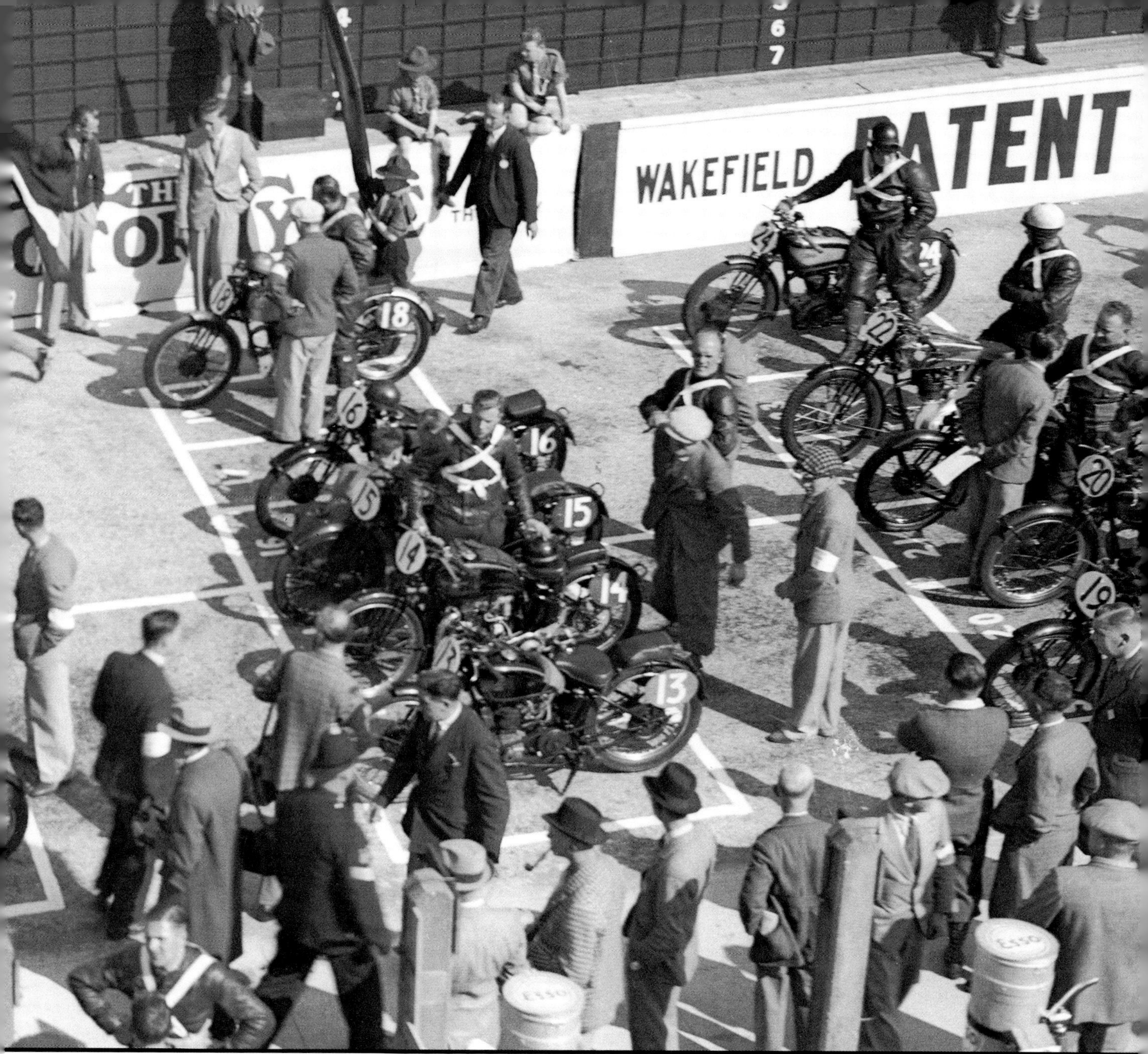
WAKEFIELD PATENT
18
16
15
14
13
24
22
20
19

An outstanding TT star of the 1930s and 1940s, short, stocky Harold Daniell wore thick-lensed spectacles that would class him unfit to be a Second World War despatch rider. After winning the 1933 Senior Manx GP on a Norton, he rode AJS in the TTs of 1934 and 1935, finishing eighth in the Junior on this bike in the latter year. After joining the Norton factory team he won the Senior TTs of 1938, 1947 and 1949.

1936

Left: John 'Crasher' White on the factory Norton he rode to second place in the Junior behind team-mate Freddie Frith. He finished fourth in the Senior. White, a biology teacher and graduate of Cambridge University, joined Norton after winning the 1934 Junior Manx GP and finished third in the 1935 Junior TT. Frequent spills in the early years led to the nickname that stuck with him until the end of his career in 1939.

Below left: Shape of things to come. The DKW ridden to third place in the Lightweight by Arthur Geiss had an unorthodox split-single two-stroke engine with reed valve induction and two main pistons with a third purely for supercharging. The open megaphone exhaust made a deafening racket that, it was claimed, could be heard on the English mainland. Geiss, from Hockenheim, had been seventh on DKW's 1935 debut.

Jimmy Guthrie made sure of winning the Senior, raising the outright lap record to 86.98mph. He had been penalised in the Junior after stopping out on the Course to replace his dislodged drive chain when leading. Officials alleged he had received outside assistance, contravening TT rules. Here he is in the Norton depot prior to the race, on his 500cc mount equipped with the company's earliest form of rear suspension, with spring plunger units.

1936

George Rowley rode an AJS in every one of his 19 TT races between 1925 and 1939. Born in the marque's home city of Wolverhampton, he moved to London to work as development engineer and rider when AJS was bought by Matchless in 1931. He finished 10th in the 1936 Junior on this 350cc overhead camshaft model, but retired in the Senior on the undeveloped air-cooled version of the AJS supercharged V4.

Stanley Woods and helper Eric Brown ready for the Senior race. Woods split the works Nortons to finish second on the latest factory Velocette, which he helped develop after arriving from Guzzi. It was one of three team machines at the TT sporting revolutionary swing-arm rear suspension with twin hydraulic units, inspired by a Dowty light aircraft undercarriage. Woods raised the lap record to 86.98mph.

1936

Stanley Woods and his wife Mildred after the maestro's Junior win on the latest 350cc Velocette, which would serve as a pattern for the company's KTT MkVIII customer racer to be released in 1939. Setting a class lap record of 85.30mph that would stand until 1950, Woods headed team-mate Mellors and Norton's Freddie Frith.

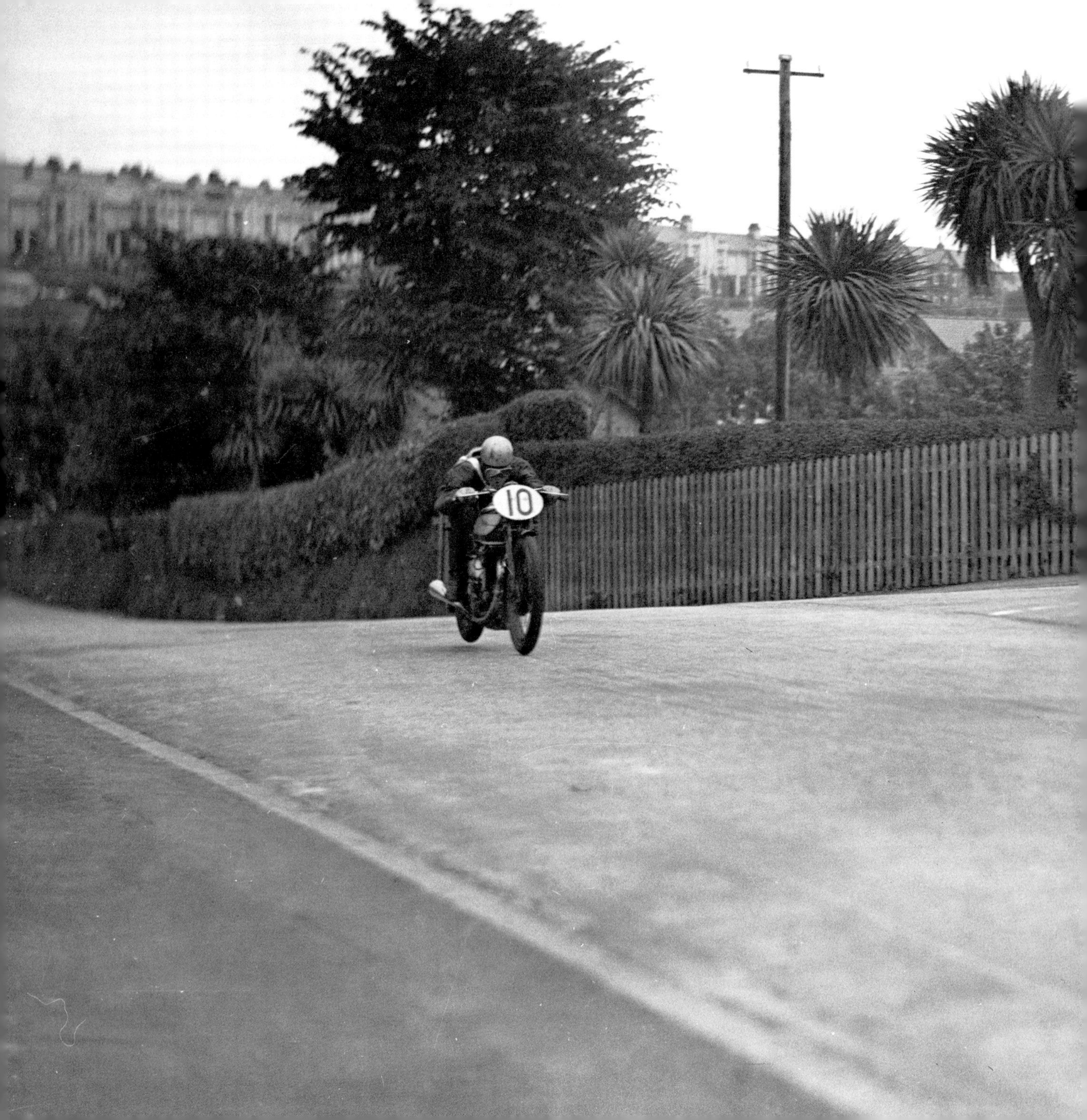
10

1936

Junior victor Freddie Frith with his Norton's rear wheel airborne on the rise following the foot of Bray Hill. A 1960s' shot taken here by photographer Nick Nicholls of 10-times TT winner Giacomo Agostini with his front wheel aloft led to this stretch of road being called Ago's Leap. Frith's first TT win was controversial: his teammate Guthrie was disqualified, then reinstated in fifth place.

America's daredevil showman Oren 'Putt' Mossman wore white leathers and entertained the paddock with his uni-cycle riding. Famous for some spectacular stunts, his TT experiences were unhappy. Putt failed to qualify on this 250cc OK Supreme in 1936, being 21 seconds outside the required 40-minute lap and on the same make again two years later he crashed at the 33rd Milestone.

1936

The HRD company founded by Howard Davies and bought by Phillip Vincent in 1928 raced its own engine at the TT from 1935. In this 1936 photo, Vincent (left) poses with his riders Jock West (on machine), Manliff Barrington, Jock Forbes and Jack Williams. West would be the team's only finisher in the Senior race. The high-camshaft engine seen here is the ancestor of the legendary postwar Vincent V-twin unit.

Isle of Man TT *The Golden Years*

1937

Right: Derbyshire-born Ted Mellors joined the Velocette team in 1936, when he took third place behind Nortons in the Junior. Here he sits on his 1937 Senior mount in the old pit lane in front of the Grandstand, where youngsters gathered behind the fence to see their heroes and collect autographs. Mellors, who had a distinguished career in TT and Grand Prix racing, took fourth place in the 500cc race, averaging 86.68mph.

Left: International sanctions imposed on Italy after the invasion of Ethiopia caused Moto Guzzi to miss the 1936 TT. Back for 1937, the factory won the Lightweight race, making Omobono Tenni the first Italian TT winner. Photographed behind the Grandstand, his 250cc single can be seen to have Guzzi's traditional horizontal cylinder and an outside flywheel. Stanley Woods, who raced a similar Guzzi, broke down on the last of the seven laps when leading.

An unusual angle on Braddan, showing Junior winner Jimmy Guthrie sweeping off the bridge. Powered by Norton's new double overhead camshaft engine, he lapped at a record 85.18mph. Guthrie led the Senior race until an engine problem forced him out at The Cutting on the Mountain climb. Two months later the popular Scot crashed at the German GP and died from his injuries. The Guthrie Memorial stands where his last TT ended..

Grimsby star Freddie Frith storms round Quarterbridge where the landmark modernist building that stands today was under construction. To be known for many years as The Nook Café, it was already being used as a grandstand. Here he races to second place behind team-mate Guthrie in the Junior. Frith made history in the Senior, winning with the first over-90mph lap, his record speed being 90.27mph.

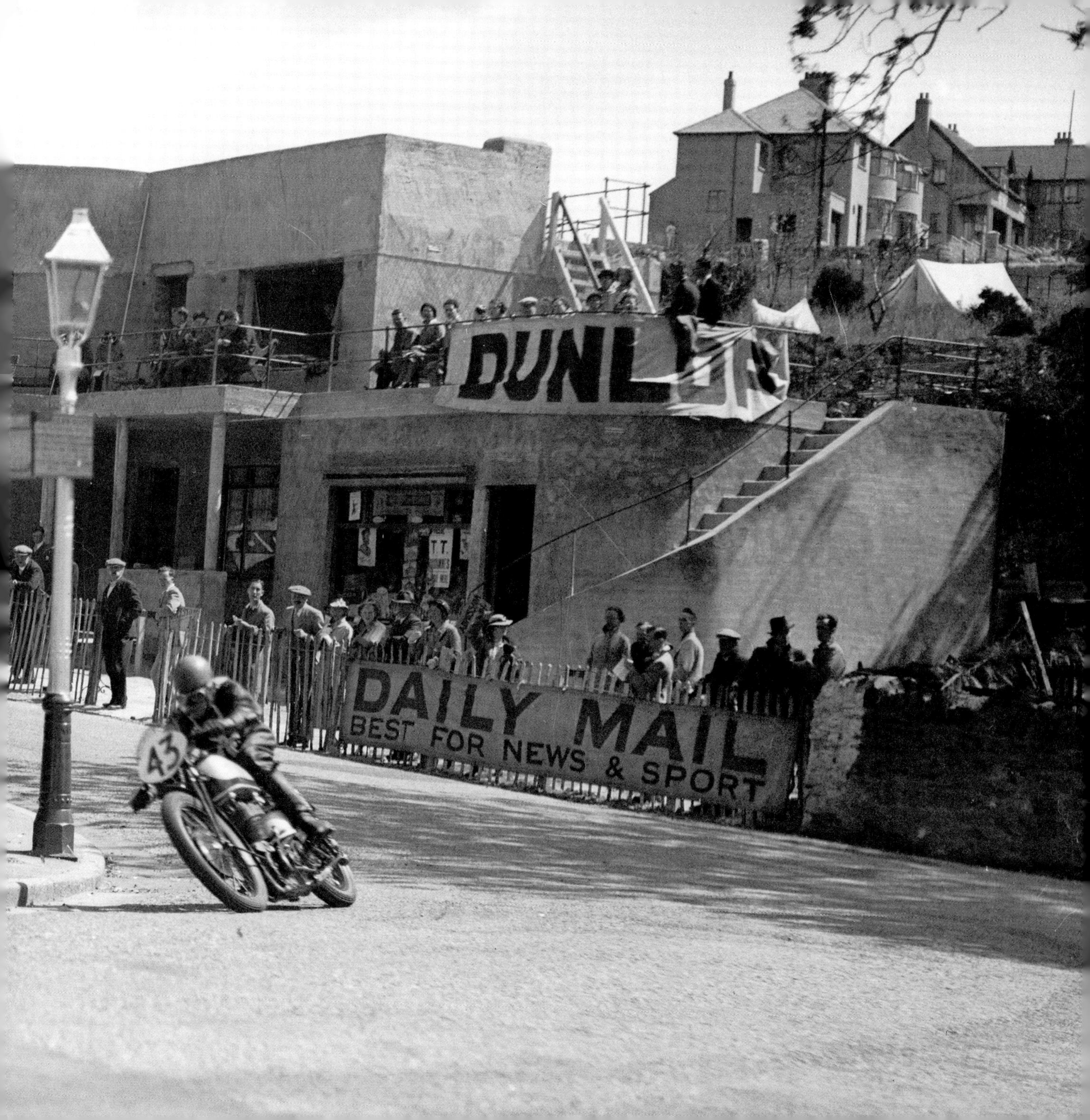
DUNL
DAILY MAIL
BEST FOR NEWS & SPORT
43

1938

Above: C B Sutherland was one of those riders who just didn't enjoy luck on the Isle of Man. He failed to finish on Nortons in 1937 Manx GP and did not start the 1938 Junior TT on this AJS after colliding with another rider and disabling a brake during the pre-race warm-up on Glencrutchery Road. The 350cc R7 AJS with chain driven camshaft is the forerunner of the better-known postwar 7R single.

Left: Noel Pope with his Junior Velocette KTT. A non-finisher in that and six other TT races, his best results were fifth places in the Senior races of 1936 and 1948. Pope's fame as a motorcyclist was not gained in the TT, but at the Brooklands circuit where he set the perpetual lap record at 124.51mph on a supercharged Brough Superior.

1938

Freddie Frith plummets through the bottom of Bray Hill on the 500cc factory Norton that carried him to third place in the 1938 Senior. Note manhole covers on the road and a spectators' grandstand in the background on the right.

Left: Karl Gall and his 500cc supercharged BMW ready for practice. Wins by the Austrian-born rider on the shaft-drive twin in the Dutch and German GPs of 1937 challenged Norton and Velocette. Gall did not make the Senior race, suffering head injuries in a spill while practising on open roads. Returning in 1939, he crashed fatally in practice and is remembered by a plaque at Ballaugh Bridge. English BMW rider Jock West is behind.

DKW clinched the Lightweight victory it had sought for three years when Ewald Kluge won on the latest supercharged two-piston 'split single' with a rotary intake valve and twin carburettors. Kluge (pronounced klooger) demolished existing 250cc records, with a lap at 80.35mph and an average of 78.48mph for seven laps. He won by more than 11 minutes, with six British ohc Excelsiors behind him.

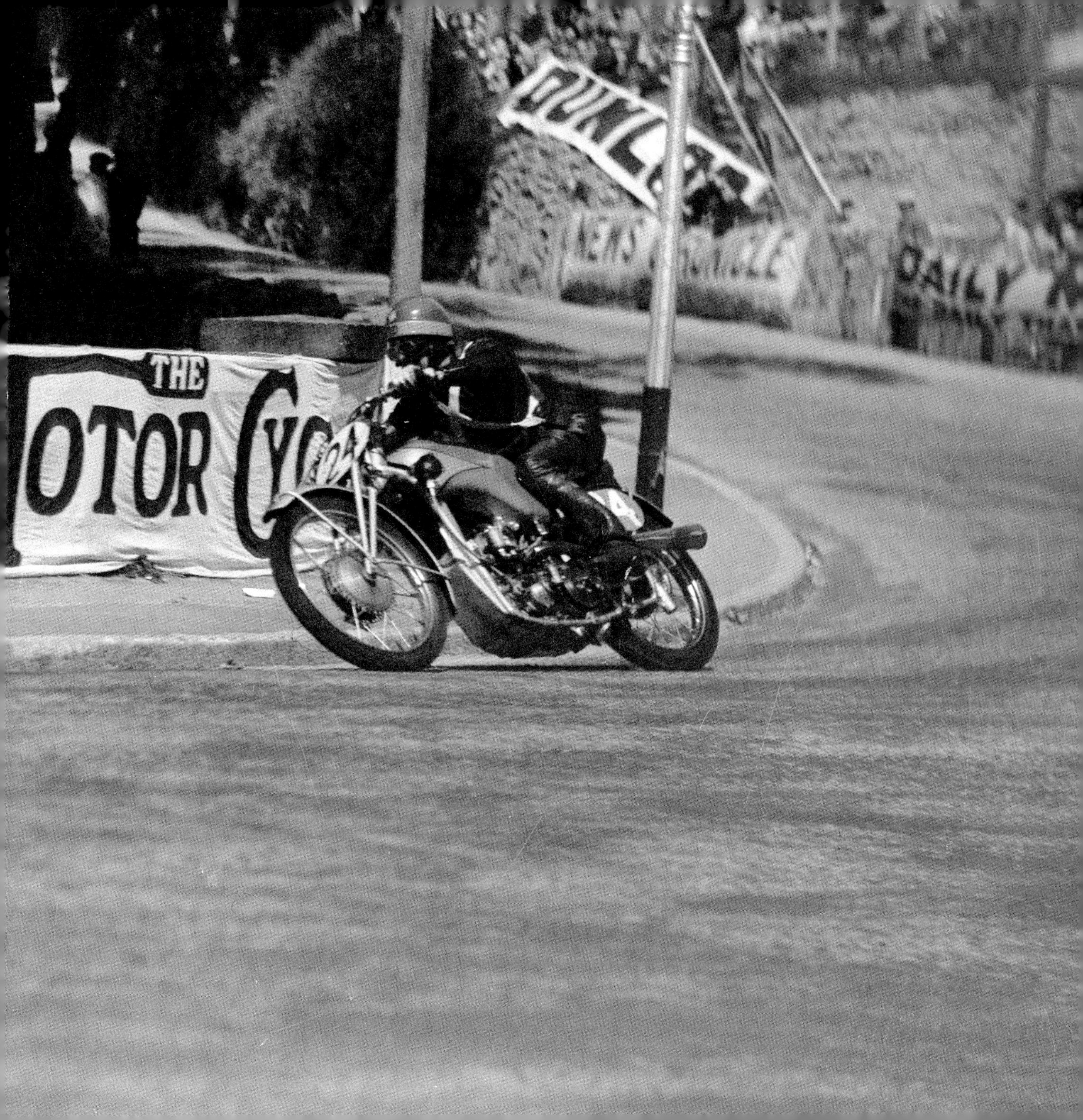
THE

Isle of Man TT *The Golden Years*

Norton's Senior team riders. Number 15 is Harold Daniell, with facial injuries from a practice crash. He won the Senior with a sensational lap record of 91.00mph that stood until the fourth postwar TT in 1950. Number 36 is John 'Crasher' White who was fourth and Number 1 is Freddie Frith who was third. Velocette's Stanley Woods was second.

1939

Fifth in the Senior race on a 1938 factory Norton, John White was a non-finisher in the Junior on this purposeful-looking 350cc NSU supercharged dohc twin. The pistol-grip fuel tank is designed to keep weight low and high-level exhaust pipes aid cornering clearance. NSU used a 500cc derivative of this engine to raise the world motorcycle speed record of 210.77mph on Bonneville Salt Flats in 1954.

1939

Winner Georg Meier, a phenomenally talented racer on loan from the Auto Union GP team, and second placeman Jock West after the Senior. Although they didn't break Harold Daniell's lap record, their BMWs dominated convincingly - and ominously, as a likely war with Germany loomed.

About to complete a BMW 1-2 in the 1939 Senior, Jock West eases round Governor's Bridge Hairpin. His Type 255 'Kompressor' has telescopic fork front suspension pioneered by BMW in 1935 (and adopted by Norton in 1938) plus plunger springing at the rear. Rider comfort helped the German machines' riders at the TT, as well as superior power and reliability.

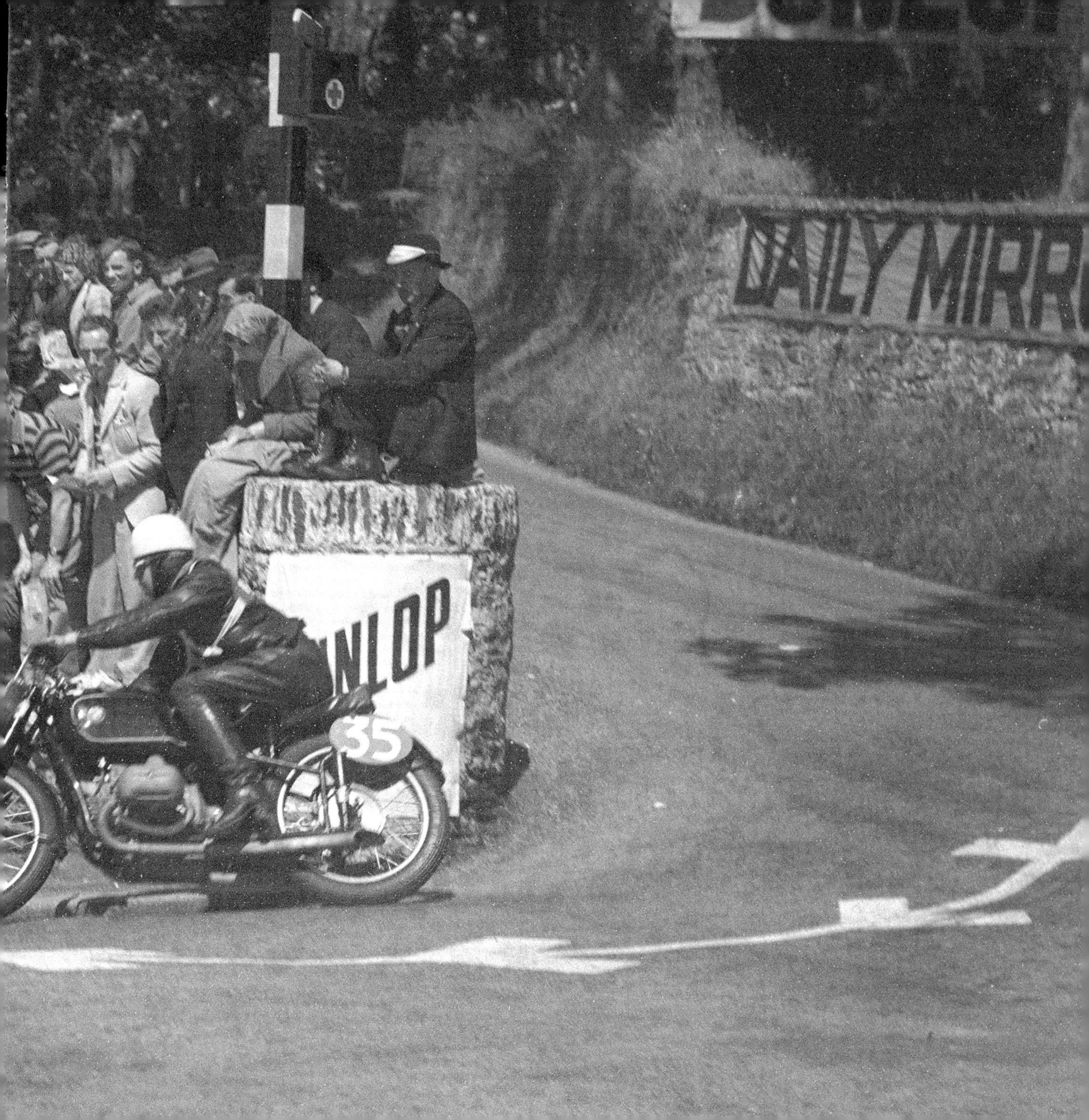
DAILY MIRR
NLOP
35

Isle of Man TT *The Golden Years*

1939

Left: Lightweight winner Ted Mellors airborne on his Italian double overhead camshaft Benelli at Ballagarraghyn, approaching Ballacraine. Keig photographers rarely ventured so far from Douglas. A coloured front numberplate and sunshine indicate a practice shot: the race was held in terrible weather. Ewald Kluge was the best of three DKW finishers in second place, while Stanley Woods (Moto Guzzi) set the fastest lap at 78.16mph before he retired.

Below: Winner Mellors at Governor's Bridge in the Lightweight. He rode a steady race on his reliable unsupercharged four-stroke to complete seven laps at 74.26mph. The winner of several Continental grands prix, Mellor had arranged the Benelli ride with the Pesaro factory, represented on the island by director Mimo Benelli and one mechanic.

Isle of Man TT *The Golden Years*

Ridden for a single practice lap by Stanley Woods, this is Velocette's innovative supercharged 500cc overhead camshaft twin, nicknamed 'The Roarer'. Set side-by-side, cylinders with contra-rotating crankshafts achieve balance and final drive is by a shaft in the frame's swing-arm. Finished shortly before the 1939 TT, this advanced machine was aimed at success in TT and GP races that never took place because of World War Two.

1939

Bob Foster on one of two AJS supercharged V4s in the Senior. Originally air-cooled, it was redesigned for 1939 with a water-cooled engine and the new frame with plunger rear suspension seen here. Results were disappointing: Foster took 13th place, while Walter Rusk was two places higher on his. Later in 1939 fearless Rusk lapped the high-speed Clady circuit in his home Ulster GP at 100mph on a four.

More about TT racing on the Isle of Man

Over the last 20 years Lily Publications has produced some of the most definitive books on this most famous of racecourses, and we have even more titles in the pipeline...

Manx Car Races – The Golden Years 1904-1953, Volume 1   96 pages, price £16.00

Published in May 2013 and written by Neil Hanson – a local Manx author who has followed car racing on the Island for many years. This book begins with a short historical account of car racing on the Isle of Man from 1904 and leads into a wide selection of historical pictures from R & L Kelly collection and that of the Keig family photographic business. Maps and other information are included to help the reader bring these stunning images to life.

Isle of Man TT – The Golden Years 1907-1939   96 pages, price £16.00

This book captures a wealth of Isle of Man historical motorcycle racing views from island photographers Keig Photographic. Many photos in this book have never been published and the collection of pictures is complemented with detailed captions written by Mick Duckworth, the renowned Manx motorbike author. Published September/October 2013.

Isle of Man TT Golden Years Series

Three further books in this series will be published by Lily Publications over the next two years. To follow on from the TT books, a series of four books will be produced on the Manx Grand Prix, all using pictures from the Keig Photographic collection.

See our website for further information on these titles.

Other TT books from Lily Publications...

Realising the Dream at the TT   A4 style, 192 pages, price £15.00

This book celebrates 50 years of road racing on the Isle of Man by Honda. Many previously unpublished pictures are included in this book which begins the story in 1959 when the Honda team travelled 6,000 miles from Japan to the Isle of Man.

Shutterspeed   128 pages, price £18.00

This book gives the reader a selection of outstanding pictures taken by local motorcyclist photographer Dave Collister with complementary text by Manx journalist and writer Mick Duckworth. A must for all TT fans.

For further details or to order any of these titles and many other Isle of Man books visit **www.lilypublications.co.uk** or contact: Lily Publications Ltd, PO Box 33, Ramsey, Isle of Man, IM99 4LP Tel: 01624 898446.